Radical Notes 3

# The US Financial Crisis

Radical Notes 3

# The US Financial Crisis

**Deepankar Basu**

AAKAR

THE US FINANCIAL CRISIS
Deepankar Basu



First Published, 2009

ISBN 978-81-89833-84-8



*Published by*
**AAKAR BOOKS**
28 E Pocket IV, Mayur Vihar Phase I, Delhi-110 091
Phone : 011-2279 5505 Telefax : 011-2279 5641
aakarbooks@gmail.com; www.aakarbooks.com

*Printed at*
Arpit Printographers, Delhi-110 032
arpitprinto@yahoo.com

A movement in a sense is a struggle over the definition of reality—how reality is constituted. It is this struggle that builds the focus and targets of the movement, informing the praxes towards social transformation. Inherent in this struggle is the act of reclaiming—sense and sensibility, words and meaning...

The word "radical", which in this post-Cold War phase of Global Capitalism or globaloney has been reduced to a general notion characterizing all kinds of extremism and deviance, is one such word that has been time and again reclaimed by the practitioners of social transformation. "Radical" derived from the Latin word, 'radix' meaning 'root' = 'basic' = 'fundamental' is a concept that aptly defines a transformatory practice as an endeavour to reveal and target the essence of what is given to us in appearance. Radicalism in this sense is nothing but fundamental transformation rather than politicking in appearances. Further, and foremost, it is the all-round critique of the status quo and its genealogies, rather than accepting the disciplinary divide/boundaries that the capitalist system perpetuates in order to control labour-power and labour, our efforts and their fruits.

***Radical Notes*** is an endeavour to coordinate the radical voices around the globe, with special focus on South Asia. In our view such focus (which could have been anything) is not just for convenience, given the facilitators' cultural and intellectual comfort, but is also needed to concretise any 'radical' pursuit. In our view South Asia provides us the opportunity to visualize the reproduction of 'global' capitalism and struggle against it in a regional setting. But we must remember such focus is always fluid with the ever-dynamic radical needs of the humanity.

***Radical Notes*** booklets are contributions on social, cultural, political or economic issues from counter-hegemonic perspectives, which need not be confined to any established socialist and communist current of thought (though these approaches are most welcome).

Series Editors
Radical Notes

# Contents


1. Introduction 7
2. Short-term Story: The Credit Freeze 12
3. The Need For Aggressive Fiscal Intervention 18
4. Medium Term Story: The Minsky Moment 22
5. The Long Term Story: Minsky After Marx 35

*References* 40

# 1

# INTRODUCTION

## THE BIG STORY

The global economic crisis currently underway is, by all accounts, the deepest economic crisis of world capitalism since the Great Depression. It was precipitated by the financial crisis that erupted in the US economy in the middle of September 2008. It is necessary for the international working class to understand the important aspects of this crisis: how it developed, the major players involved, the instruments used during the speculative build-up leading up to the crisis and the possible consequences of these events for the working people of the world. This understanding is necessary to formulate a socialist, i.e., working class, response to these earth shaking events.

The current crisis can possibly be fruitfully understood if the unfolding events are measured against different time scales: the short-term, i.e., in terms of days and weeks; the medium-term, i.e., in terms of months and years; and the long-term, i.e., in terms of decades. This analytical compartmentalization into three different time periods is useful because it demonstrates how long-term trends silently but inexorably created the conditions for the medium-term problem to explode into the short-term problem that has buffeted the economy since mid-September, 2008.

In the short-term, the current financial meltdown is a severe credit crisis, a situation where financial institutions have become unwilling or unable to lend and borrow among themselves, thereby freezing the flow of credit in the entire economic system; this credit freeze is largely the result of a serious loss of faith in financial institutions and possibly also in the whole financial system and came to the fore most forcefully in the middle of September, 2008. It is also possible that the credit freeze, and the underlying loss of faith, might explode into a full-blown banking crisis: banking panic leading to run on even healthy and solvent banks.

Looked at from a medium-term perspective, the crisis is the unraveling of an extremely large leveraged speculative bubble on Us real estate that built itself up for about seven years from the beginning of this decade (and century); this speculative bubble spawned fancy financial instruments fashioned by Wall Street operators, running all the way from sub-prime mortgages, asset backed securities (ABS) and mortgage backed securities (MBS), collateralized debt obligations (CDO) to credit default swaps (CDS); this speculative bubble led up to and culminated, when it finally burst in the middle of 2007, in the credit crisis that the US, and gradually the global, economy found itself in.

From a longer term perspective the present crisis is, of course, more than just about Wall Street and finance and banking; it is a full-blown crisis of the neoliberal turn in capitalism inaugurated during the 1970s. Neoliberalism (or more correctly, the neoliberal counterrevolution) was a response to the structural crisis of capitalism that emerged in the late 1960s. It was a response from the point of view of the upper fraction of the capitalist class, a fraction especially dominated by financial interests. The neoliberal counterrevolution ushered in a capitalism firmly under the sway of finance capital; and the neoliberal policy turn was geared towards breaking the power of labour vis-a-vis capital that had gradually built up during the two decades after World War II and restoring the revenues and social power of capital. The result of the neoliberal turn was stagnant real wages, slow but growing productivity, and hence growing profit incomes - especially of the financial sector - and increasing financialization and a deregulated economy for finance to operate in.

Stagnant wages created the demand for debt from a working class used to ever-growing consumption spending; huge profit incomes and the shredding of all regulation on finance created the supply. The result was a growing role of debt in the lives of the working class which, over time, led to a huge debt overhang on the entire economy. As the ratio of outstanding debt to income rose, a direct result of stagnant incomes for the majority, the financial fragility of the entire system increased; and it is this systemically fragile financial architecture that finally cracked under the weight of the bursting housing bubble. Thus, the long-term build-up of debt in the US economy resulting from the neoliberal counterrevolution increased the financial fragility of the system and created the conditions in which the bursting of various asset price bubbles could lead to a severe credit crisis and loss of faith in the entire financial system.

The result of the financial meltdown could be a very severe recession in the US economy. Real GDP figures released by the US Bureau of Economic Analysis (BEA) on October 30, 2008 indicated that the US economy was in the midst of a slowdown even before the financial storm hit the world economy in the middle of September[1]. Real GDP in the US contracted at an annual rate of 0.3 percent for the third quarter (i.e., for the months of July, August and September), led by a sharp fall in consumer spending as can be seen from Table 1. The financial storm, comprising a severe credit crisis and even a possible banking crisis, will only deepen the slowdown and might even push the US and the rest of the world into a prolonged and painful recession, possibly even a decade long L-shaped recession like the one that Japan witnessed during the lost decade of the 1990s. During such recessions it is the working class which bears the brunt of the whole slowdown with unemployment rates rising, median duration of

1. http://www.bea.gov/newsreleases/national/gdp/gdpnewsrelease.htm

**TABLE 1 : Percent Change from Last Period (Real GDP, US)**

| | *2007-I* | *2007-II* | *2007-III* | *2007-IV* | *2008-I* | *2008-II* | *2008-III* |
|---|---|---|---|---|---|---|---|
| **Gross domestic product** | **0.1** | **4.8** | **4.8** | **– 0.2** | **0.9** | **2.8** | **– 0.3** |
| **Personal consumption expenditures** | **3.9** | **2** | **2** | **1** | **0.9** | **1.2** | **– 3.1** |
| Durable goods | 9.2 | 5 | 2.3 | 0.4 | – 4.3 | – 2.8 | – 14.1 |
| Nondurable goods | 3.5 | 1.9 | 1.2 | 0.3 | – 0.4 | 3.9 | – 6.4 |
| Services | 3.1 | 1.4 | 2.4 | 1.4 | 2.4 | 0.7 | 0.6 |
| **Gross private domestic investment** | **– 9.6** | **6.2** | **3.5** | **– 11.9** | **– 5.8** | **– 11.5** | **– 1.9** |
| Fixed investment | – 3.4 | 3 | – 0.9 | – 6.2 | – 5.6 | – 1.7 | – 5.6 |
| Nonresidential | 3.4 | 10.3 | 8.7 | 3.4 | 2.4 | 2.5 | – 1 |
| Structures | 11.2 | 18.3 | 20.5 | 8.5 | 8.6 | 18.5 | 7.9 |
| Equipment and software | 0 | 6.9 | 3.6 | 1 | – 0.6 | – 5 | – 5.5 |
| Residential | – 16.2 | – 11.5 | – 20.6 | – 27 | – 25.1 | – 13.3 | – 19.1 |
| Change in private inventories | | | | | | | |
| **Net exports of goods and services** | | | | | | | |
| Exports | 0.6 | 8.8 | 23 | 4.4 | 5.1 | 12.3 | 5.9 |
| Goods | 2.1 | 6.9 | 21.8 | 5.1 | 4.5 | 16.3 | 7.5 |
| Services | – 2.7 | 13.3 | 25.9 | 2.7 | 6.4 | 3.8 | 2.3 |
| Imports | 7.7 | – 3.7 | 3 | – 2.3 | – 0.8 | –7.3 | – 1.9 |
| Goods | 8.4 | – 4 | 2.4 | – 2.6 | – 2 | – 7.1 | – 2.8 |
| Services | 4.2 | – 2 | 6.3 | – 0.9 | 5.5 | – 8 | 3.5 |
| **Government consumption expenditures and gross investment** | **0.9** | **3.9** | **3.8** | **0.8** | **1.9** | **3.9** | **5.8** |
| Federal | – 3.6 | 6.7 | 7.2 | -0.5 | 5.8 | 6.6 | 13.8 |
| National defense | – 5.9 | 8.5 | 10.2 | -0.9 | 7.3 | 7.3 | 18.1 |
| Nondefense | 1.2 | 3.1 | 1.2 | 0.4 | 2.9 | 5 | 4.8 |
| State and local | 3.6 | 2.4 | 1.9 | 1.6 | -0.3 | 2.5 | 1.4 |

*Source*: http://www.bea.gov/

unemployment increasing and wage incomes either stagnating or falling. In such a scenario, fixing the financial mess, dealing with the credit freeze, averting a possible run on the commercial banking system and restoring confidence in the financial system will not be enough to prevent a plunge into a deep, prolonged and painful recession; addressing the credit crisis is necessary but not sufficient to deal with the grave crisis in the real sector. An aggressive fiscal intervention by the US government and other governments around the world, in terms of direct expenditure on goods and services, will be necessary to prevent the slide into a prolonged recession. It is in the interests of the working class to push for such interventions even as it works towards rebuilding its political, social and economic institutions to work for its longer term goal of building a socialist society.

# 2

# SHORT-TERM STORY: THE CREDIT FREEZE

## The Sequence of Events

Even though the credit crisis attained dangerous proportions only in mid-September, it had already announced itself in the early part of the year with the collapse of Bear Stearns, one of the five famed investment banks that defined Wall Street. Faced with a fierce run on its dwindling reserves and its stock plummeting, Bears Stearns was forced to sell itself off to J P Morgan Chase (one of the largest commercial banks in the US) on March 16, 2008. The next three months could be best described in terms that the police often use in India: tense but under control. On July 01, the next piece of bad news emerged: Country Wide Financials, the largest mortgage seller in the US, collapsed and was acquired by Bank of America (again, one of the largest commercial banks in the US). Following closely on the heels of this event, IndyMac bank failed - the second largest bank failure in US history - and was taken over by the Federal Deposit Insurance Corporation (FDIC), one of the institutions responsible for monitoring the health of the banking system in the US. IndyMac was, quite unsurprisingly, part of the Country Wide financial family.

Things started really speeding up in September. On September 08, Freddie Mac and Fannie Mae, the two giant government supported enterprises (GSE) in the mortgage market had to be nationalized, with assets of the two entities totaling more than $ 5 trillion. On September 15 another of the five famed investment banks, Lehmann Brothers, filed for bankruptcy; Lehmann's assets were a little over 600 billion dollars and this made its bankruptcy filing the largest in US history. Next day, the Fed stepped in with a $ 85 billion loan to prevent American International Group (AIG), the largest insurance firm in the US, from going under. These two events, Lehmann's bankruptcy filing and AIG's rescue, sent shock waves through the world financial system. The result was a rapid erosion of faith in the financial system leading to a severe credit freeze: financial institutions stopped lending, to other financial institutions, to businesses and to consumers. We will return to these events later, after we have narrated the medium term story, and look at them once again in greater detail.

The next thirty six hours, from the morning of September 17 to the evening of September 18, accelerated the credit crisis to dangerous proportions and convinced the US Treasury and the Federal Reserve that government intervention of unheard magnitudes (at least since the Great Depression) would be necessary to prevent total financial collapse. Ben Bernanke, the chairman of the Federal Reserve (the US Central Bank), was famously reported as saying, at one point during this 36 hour period, that if the government did not save the (financial) markets now there might not be any financial markets in the future. So, what happened during these crucial 36 hours?

**The Crucial 36 Hours**

The first indication of a severe stress in the financial system was a shooting up of credit default swap (CDS) rates, especially in Morgan Stanley and Goldman Sachs (two of the famed five Wall Street investment banks). Credit default swaps are insurance contracts that can protect bondholders against the possibility of default. For example if an investor has bought bonds worth $ 1 million issued by firm A, then the investor can also buy CDS - typically issued by financial institutions like large commercial banks, investment banks or insurance companies - to protect herself against a possible loss resulting from firm A defaulting on its bonds; the premium that the investor pays for the CDS is called the "rate" or "spread" and has typically been around 2% of the amount insured (what is known as the "notional value"). So, in this case, the investor would pay $ 20,000 to buy CDS and if firm A were to go under, then the "counterparty" to the CDS contract (i.e., the financial institution that issued the CDS to the investor) would step in to pay the investor the amount of her loss resulting from the holding of firm A bonds. Thus, CDS rates, being in essence insurance premium rates, are an indication of the market's belief about the possibility of default of the institution on which the CDS are written; CDS rates on bonds issued by firms are typically low when the market thinks the probability of default of those firms are low and high when the market thinks the probability of default is high. Thus, on the morning of September 17, when CDS rates went through the roof, this provided evidence of a soaring expectation of major defaults in the financial system. Investors' awareness of increased probabilities of default resulted in a severe loss of faith in a wide range of private financial instruments.

When investors lose faith in the financial instruments issued by private parties, they turn back to those issued by the government and that is what happened when CDS rates multiplied by close to a factor of five. Investors let go of private financial instruments like hot bricks and rushed into US government securities, a phenomenon often described in the financial press as a "flight to safety". The US government, i.e., the US Treasury department, primarily issues three kinds of securities (i.e., financial instruments): T-bills, T-notes and T-bonds (where the "T" stands for Treasury), where bills are financial instruments that mature in less than a year, notes mature between one and ten years and bonds are of longer maturities than a decade. When investors lost faith in the private financial system, they rushed in to US T-bills; shorter maturity instruments are preferred by investors because of their flexibility. This huge rush into T-bills pushed up the price of T-bills and drove the yield (i.e., interest rate) on T-bills down; prices of bonds are inversely related to their yields, so that when prices rise the yields fall. At one point in time the yield on T-bills were zero (the lowest it can ever go to) implying that investors were willing to hold T-bills even though the nominal return was zero and real returns were negative (because the inflation rate was positive).

As private investors were madly rushing into the safety of US T-bills, another important event was unfolding in the mutual funds market. Money market mutual funds (MMMF) are financial institutions that have become popular over the last three decades, especially in the US. They typically work as follows: investors put their money in MMMF's by purchasing shares in the MMMF's stock; thus the MMMF acts as a mechanism for pooling huge amounts of money and then using those large sums for investing in extremely diversified portfolios of financial assets. Diversification reduces the riskiness of investment substantially and so investing in MMMFs was, till September 17, thought to be as safe as a holding one's money in a deposit account in a commercial bank; the added advantage was that the money invested in MMMF shares would give a positive rate of return as opposed to a deposit account which is usually non-interest bearing. On September 17, one of the oldest and largest MMMFs, Reserve Primary Fund, "broke the buck", i.e., it made losses on its investments to such an extent that it could not guarantee a positive return to its shareholders. This was an unheard of event in recent financial history and as news of Reserve Primary Fund's losses spread, investors started pulling money out of MMMFs.

This had a very negative consequence for the real economy because of the serious involvement of MMMFs in the commercial paper (CP) market[2]. Businesses typically need to constantly borrow short-term funds to keep its operations going; these funds go towards funding payroll, paying suppliers, maintaining inventory etc. Firms usually borrow short-term funds in the US by issuing commercial paper (a bond with a short maturity), the private counterpart of T-bills. Who buys commercial papers? The most active

2. See http://www.dollarsandsense.org/archives/2008/1008wolff.html for more details

institutional investors in the CP market are the MMMFs; some of the largest chunks of commercial papers are bought by the MMMFs. So when the MMMFs faced an increasing spate of withdrawal, in the wake of Reserve Primary Fund's breaking the buck, they stopped buying commercial paper. This, essentially, meant that the CP market ground to a halt. Thus businesses were no longer able to borrow the short-term funds that they need to keep operating. The economy, by all means, shut down.

Adding to and going hand-in-hand with these processes were the growing problems in the interbank (lending) market. Commercial banks typically lend and borrow banking system reserves (roughly the sum of currency in the commercial banks' vaults and the amount they hold in their accounts with the Central Bank) among themselves for very short, usually overnight, periods. The interbank lending market that is most closely watched is the London interbank market and the rate at which loans are made in this market is the London Inter Bank Offered Rate (LIBOR). The most important characteristic of these loans, for the purposes of this story, is that they are unsecured, i.e., they are not backed by collateral. Thus, a bank can get a loan in the interbank market only if other banks consider it financially sound; thus when the LIBOR increases it provides evidence that the largest and the best banks in the world had lost faith on each other. On September 17, the LIBOR shot up, giving indication of increasing strain in the interbank market.

It was these sets of events - CDS rates shooting up, closing down of the CP market, increasing strain in the interbank market - that spooked the US administration and convinced them of the necessity of the most extensive government intervention in the financial markets since the Great Depression. These crucial sets of events were precipitated by the string of big financial failures that the US economy witnessed over the first two weeks of September: the near-failure and subsequent nationalization of Fannie and Freddie, the bankruptcy of Lehmann Brothers and the near-collapse and costly rescue of AIG. It was these failures, and more so the hidden implications of these failures, that led to a rapid loss of faith in the financial system.

But why were Fannie and Freddie nationalized, why did Lehmann and AIG fail? The short answer is that these financial institutions failed because at crucial points in time they could no longer raise money from the market to finance their assets, i.e., they could not borrow money. And why did financing dry up for these big and reputed financial institutions? Because each of these, in its own way, was exposed to the subprime mortgage market and the leveraged speculation that built around it, and thus took huge losses when the subprime mortgage market started unraveling.

# 3

# THE NEED FOR AGGRESSIVE FISCAL INTERVENTION

Before we move on to looking at the global economic crisis from a medium term perspective, i.e., before we take a look at the phenomenon of the house price bubble and associated speculation that created the grounds for the current credit crisis, it might not be amiss to focus on what can be done in the short-run to deal with the real consequences of the economic crisis: the deep and prolonged recession that the US economy will undoubtedly be pushed into. Real GDP figures released by the US Bureau of Economic Analysis (BEA) on October 30, 2008, as I have already suggested earlier, indicated in no uncertain terms that the US economy was in the midst of a slowdown even *before* the financial storm hit the world economy in the middle of September. Real GDP in the US contracted at an annual rate of 0.3 percent for the third quarter (i.e., for the months of July, August and September), led by a sharp fall in consumer spending; businesses cut 240,000 jobs in October alone, the highest figure in 14 years[3]; retail sales fell by record levels in the US October, 2008[4]. As I have indicated above, the only sensible way to deal with the looming recession is

---

3. http://www.canada.com/victoriatimescolonist/news/story.html?id=407baf10-cc72-4e8c-b407-b0caef9030b7
4. http://www.nytimes.com/2008/11/15/business/economy/15econ.html?_r=1&oref=slogin

injection of aggregate demand through direct government expenditure. Why is that so?

In any capitalist economy, such as the US economy, the level of aggregate economic activity and employment is determined, in the short run, by the level of aggregate demand, and fluctuations in employment and output are accordingly determined by fluctuations of aggregate demand. Aggregate demand is defined as the sum total of all expenditures on goods and services produced in the economy. Macroeconomists divide total expenditure that make up aggregate demand into four distinct categories: consumption expenditure, investment expenditure, government expenditure and net export expenditure. Consumption expenditure is the total spending by households on durable and non-durable goods, and also services; investment expenditure is the total spending by firms on plant, equipment, machinery and inventories, and the residential investment expenditures by households; government expenditure includes the total spending by local, state and federal government agencies on goods and services (excluding transfer payments); and net export expenditure is the net amount that foreigners spend on buying goods and services produced in the domestic economy.

BEA figures released for the third quarter show that every component of aggregate demand emanating from the private sector of the US (or foreign) economy either declined or slowed down when compared to the second quarter. In real terms, consumption expenditure decreased by 3.1 percent, the steepest decline since 1980 when the US economy was in the grip of a severe recession; during the previous recession in 2001, consumption expenditures had not even declined. Investment expenditures, other than those devoted to maintaining inventories, have also declined. Real nonresidential fixed investment expenditures decreased 1.0 percent in the third quarter, in contrast to an increase of 2.5 percent in the second. Expenditures on nonresidential structures increased by 7.9 percent, compared with a much higher increase of 18.5 percent in the last quarter; expenditures on equipment and software decreased 5.5 percent. Real residential fixed investment decreased 19.1 percent, compared with a decrease of 13.3 percent in the second quarter. Demand emanating from the external sector has a similar story to tell: even though exports registered a positive growth, the growth had slowed down considerably falling from 12.3 to 5.9 percent.

This is hardly surprising. With credit drying up, home equity vanishing and layoffs increasing, working-class households cannot be expected to increase their expenditures on the purchase of goods and services; a continued decline in the stock markets, coupled with increasing volatility will make matters worse. A recent survey in the US showed that consumer confidence was at its lowest value in 40 years, and so it is almost certain that consumption expenditure will not rise in the foreseeable future. Neither will export expenditures rise to shore up aggregate demand because most of the economies in the world are either already into a recession or are rapidly slowing down. Nor can firms be expected to increase their expenditures on plant and machinery and equipment. And the problem here is more than a credit freeze: even if the credit markets were to ease due to government intervention, which it is adamantly refusing to do, firms might not be willing to expand their operations because they face sagging demand. Capitalist firms produce to make profits; if they expect markets to be down and demand to fall, they will cut back and not increase their expenditures even if the cost of financing goes down.

That leaves us with government expenditure as the only source for increasing aggregate demand. In the midst of possibly the worst economic crisis since the Great Depression, the US government needs to aggressively step up its expenditure on goods and services; since private expenditures, either of firms or of households, cannot be expected to increase in the short-term, aggressive fiscal intervention seems to be the only way the US government can prevent the economy from sliding into a decade long L-shaped recession that was Japan's fate in the 1990s. Moreover, such expenditures are warranted even from a long-term perspective of economic growth. Rebuilding the crumbling public infrastructure like roads and bridges, improving and widening the ambit of the public transport systems in US cities, jump-starting the movement towards green technologies, making health care available to all working-class Americans, increasing the unemployment benefit substantially, investing in the educational infrastructure makes both short-term and long-term sense. It will help boost aggregate demand in the short run and prevent a slide into a prolonged recession, and in the long run it will build the physical and human capital to help take the US economy into a higher growth trajectory.

Two alternatives to boost the economy, which are often brought up in this context, also seem to have lost their efficacy: tax breaks and monetary policy. Tax breaks have already been tried out and does not seem to have worked; reeling under mountains of debt, the tax break (or refund) cheque is often used by households not for making new purchases but for reducing the outstanding debt. The second alternative, monetary policy action, is also rapidly reaching the point where it will become totally ineffective. For it is almost certain now that the US economy is already stuck in what John Maynard Keynes long ago called a liquidity trap, a situation where the Central Bank can no longer boost aggregate demand by reducing interest rates. The Fed has already reduced the target federal funds rate to 1 percent and reducing it further to 0 percent, the lowest it can go, will possibly not help. Even if confidence in the financial system is restored and nominal interest rates lowered, this might not increase borrowing by firms because of their bleak forecast of falling demand for the goods they produce. Monetary policy has reached its limits; the only option to ward off a severe recession and increase the pain on the working class seems to be aggressive fiscal intervention in terms of direct expenditure on goods and services by the US government.

# 4

# MEDIUM TERM STORY: THE MINSKY MOMENT

## The Housing Bubble

The medium term story of the evolving financial crisis begins at the end of the last century. With the bursting of the dot-com bubble at the end of the 1990s, possibilities of a long recession hovered on the horizon. The Federal Reserve, the Central Bank of the US, moved in with the tools of monetary policy to ease the slowdown. The (effective) federal funds rate, the key short-term interest rate that the Fed monitors as part of it's monetary policy tasks, gradually moved down from over 6 percent per annum to a little below 2 percent within a span of about an year as the chart below shows. Lowering interest rates to engineer a soft-landing for a slowing economy is a natural thing to do: reducing the cost of borrowing funds is a key way the Central Bank can affect the level of investment and consumption (especially of durable goods) expenditures and thereby boost the level of aggregate demand in a slowing capitalist economy. With finance in command, this normal and natural move had a perverse effect.

The effects of the falling federal funds rate gradually cascaded from the short-end to the longer end of the asset market, lowering interest rates on all kinds of contracts. One of the key long-term interest rates affected by this very sensible move of the Fed was the interest rate charged on various kinds of mortgage loans (loans to finance the purchase

**FIGURE 1 : US FED FUNDS RATE (EFFECTIVE)**

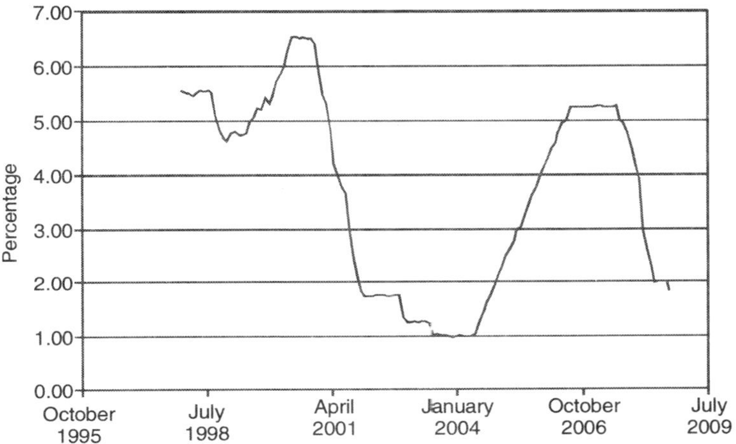


of homes). With mortgage interest rates falling, consumers not only started purchasing new homes with new mortgage loans but also refinancing their old mortgages. With the demand for mortgage loans increasing, and the increase sustained by a low-interest rate regime, house prices started picking up. Very soon, i.e., within a year or two, economists started noticing a bubble in house prices. There were several indicators of a house price bubble. For instance, the Case-Shiller house price index for 10 US cities - a commonly used price index for houses - increased rapidly since the early 2000s, as Figure 2 shows. Even more tellingly, the price-to-rental ratio of houses went through the roof. Between January 2000 and April 2006, the rental of an average house did not increase at all; during the same period, price of an average house increased by about 70 percent, sending the price-to-rental ratio on an upward spiral, as noted by Paul Krugman[5].

5. See http://krugman.blogs.nytimes.com/2008/10/02/bad-ideas/

**FIGURE 2 : CASE-SHILLER COMPOSITE HOUSE PRICE INDEX (10 US CITIES)**

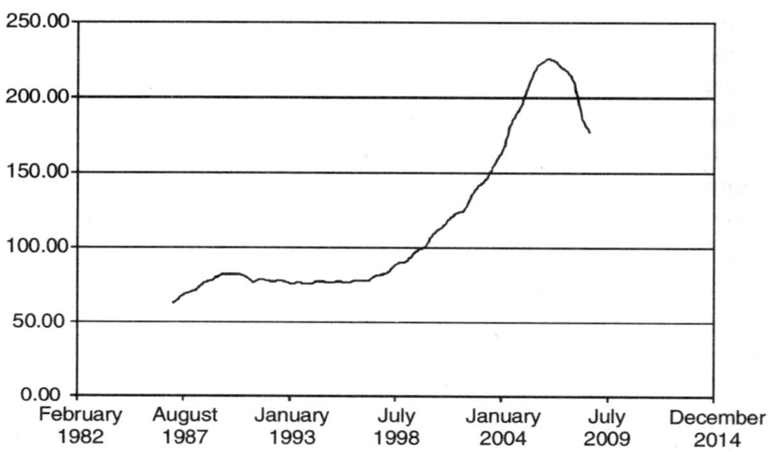


The fact that the price-to-rental ratio increased rapidly gave a clear indication that a house price bubble was building up. People were, in other words, purchasing houses not because of the service provided by a house but because of speculative motives. A rough proxy for the value attributed by consumers to the service provided by a house is the rental rate; since this was not increasing, it meant that people were not valuing the real service provided by the house. But prices of houses were shooting up giving an indication of an increasing demand for houses (relative to supply). Most of this demand was clearly arising from speculative motives; many of the house purchases were for the purpose of selling them off at a later date to reap capital gains (i.e., the profit derived from the difference between the selling and the buying price of the asset). Thus, the rise in prices was not driven by "fundamentals" (i.e., increase in the intrinsic value of the service provided by houses) but largely by speculative motives of capital gains; that is precisely what leads to an asset price bubble and that is what happened.

## The Subprime Mortgage Market

A run of a couple of quarters of rising house prices was very soon incorporated into the expectation formation mechanisms of financial markets. As has been observed over and over again in history, rising asset prices very soon creates irrational expectations that prices will keep rising, rising certainly in the foreseeable future if not forever. Such periods of rapidly rising expectations, feeding primarily on itself, have been labelled as "manias" by economists studying periods of asset price boom-and-bust. Prominent examples of such economists are Charles P. Kindleberger and Hyman P. Minsky, coming, as they are, from very different political traditions. In the context of the early twenty-first century US economy, the unprecedented house price bubble created grounds for the emergence of predatory lending and the sub-prime mortgage market. The sub-prime mortgage market was the market for mortgage loans to less-than-creditworthy borrowers at very high interest rates that often came with hidden but onerous terms[6].

A financial innovation that indirectly helped the emerging sub-prime mortgage market and the practice of predatory lending was "securitization". Securitization, in the context of the mortgage market, meant pooling together hundreds and thousands of mortgage loans together and then selling bonds on that pool of mortgages. Investors buying those bonds - the mortgage backed bonds - received the income stream, both the principal and the interest, entailed by the mortgages as the mortgage borrowers serviced their debt. Securitization required that the entities, usually investment banks like Bear Stearns or Merril Lynch, that were issuing (i.e., selling) mortgage backed securities (the mortgage backed bonds or other kinds of assets backed by the mortgage pool) needed ownership of the pool of mortgages against which those mortgage backed securities were being issued. Thus, the entities that issued the mortgage backed securities went out and bought mortgage loans from the originators of the mortgages, i.e., those who sold the mortgage loan to the

6. Useful material on predatory lending and the subprime mortgage market can be found here: http://www.dollarsandsense.org/predatorylending.html

borrower, like Country Wide Financial (the largest mortgage seller in the US prior to the financial collapse).

The fact that mortgage loan originators had a market where they could sell off the mortgage loans they had originated created perverse incentives for the originators. Typically mortgage loan originators do a thorough screening to assess the financial background of applicants before making loans. With the emerging market for selling off mortgages, the effort at screening was reduced to zero. Things actually went even further. Since mortgages could be sold off at good prices to the investment banks, the mortgage loan originators had a incentive to start engaging in predatory lending, i.e., push mortgage loans on persons who they knew would not be able to sustain the payments entailed by the loan. Since the originator did not have to bear the risk of failure associated with non-payment of mortgage loans, they had no incentive to make prudent loans. All they had to do was to force some gullible working class person to agree to the sub-prime loan and then turn around and sell it off to some investment bank in Wall Street. Thus, the market for sub-prime mortgages proliferated, driven by rising demand coming from the Wall Street investment banks. And why were investment banks so eager to buy these sub-prime mortgages? To answer this question, let us look a little more closely at the process and results of "securitization".

## Securitization: Slice, Dice, and Repackage

Securitization is the division, repackaging and dispersal of debt, earning huge fee income for the entity (usually an investment bank) that is undertaking this process. The process starts with some commercial or investment bank buying a swathe of mortgages, some prime, some sub-prime, from smaller financial institutions and pooling them together. Each mortgage, recall, entails a stream of future payments; so the pool of mortgages, entails some specific stream of future payments. Various categories or "tranches" of bonds, arranged according to their risk characteristics, are then issued against the pool of underlying mortgages, i.e., against the stream of future payments entailed by the pool of mortgages. Investors who buy these bonds (mortgage backed securities) then have the claims on the mortgage payments coming through month after month after month; if some mortgage fails i.e., payments stop the lowest category (i.e., most risky) bondholder loses first, the losses traveling up the tier of the bonds. The whole edifice, of course, was built of extremely shaky foundations: sub-prime loans to people whose incomes were sagging, as Figure 3 demonstrates.

**FIGURE 3 : SHAKY FOUNDATIONS**

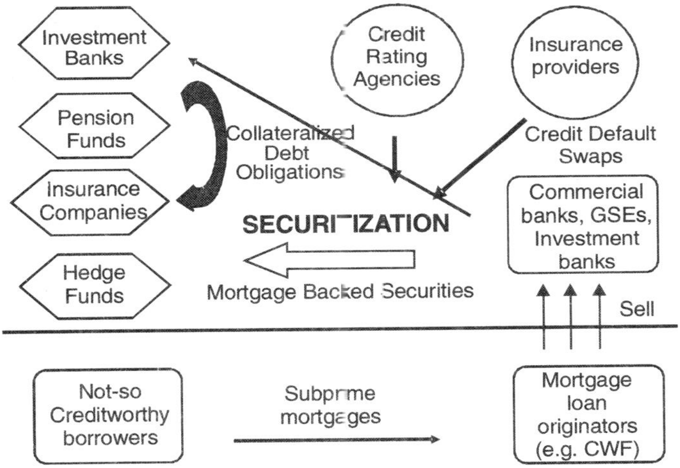

Investment Banks
Pension Funds
Insurance Companies
Hedge Funds
Credit Rating Agencies
Insurance providers
Collateralized Debt Obligations
Credit Default Swaps
SECURITIZATION
Commercial banks, GSEs, Investment banks
Mortgage Backed Securities
Sell
Not-so Creditworthy borrowers
Subprime mortgages
Mortgage loan originators (e.g. CWF)

Let us look at a specific example: Bear Stearns Alt-A Mortgage Pass-Through Certificate. This is how this mortgage backed security worked. Bear Stearns bought 2871 mortgages from different mortgage originators for a total of $1.3 billion; this mortgage pool had mortgages that had been originated in different parts of the US, each worth on average for $ 450,000. Bear Stearns then pooled these diverse mortgages and issued 37 different bonds against that pool of mortgages; these bonds were called the Alt-A Mortgage Pass-Through Certificates. Alt-A stands for a very specific kind of mortgage: a mortgage where the originator does not ask any questions about the financial situation of the borrower before making the loan. It is not even ascertained whether the person taking the loan has a stable employment or not!

Two additional players come into the picture: credit rating agencies and insurance companies. Since many investors had an idea that the mortgage backed bonds were risky investments, they required some "independent" rating agency like Standard & Poor's or Moody's to ascertain the riskiness associated with investing in those bonds. This is one of the typical functions of credit rating agencies[7]: to ascertain the riskiness (i.e., risk of default) of bonds and assign a credit rating to it; credit ratings run from AAA/Aaa (least risky) to C/D (in default). There were two problems with the involvement of credit rating agencies in the whole securitization process. First, there was an acute shortage of reliable information about the mortgages in the underlying pool; recall how the mortgages in the pool had originated in very different geographical locations, had been offered to very different income categories of people. Most importantly, very little information was collected about the financial standing of the borrowers (especially in Alt-A mortgages). So, despite their best efforts, the credit rating agencies could not come up with realistic risk assessment of the bonds issued against the pool of mortgages. The second problem was even more serious: a conflict of interest. Who paid the fees to the credit rating agencies? The same investment banks that issued the mortgage backed bonds; thus, there was a real incentive for the rating agencies to underplay the risk and certify most of the bonds as "investment grade". That is more or less what happened, as we now know.

The other player in the securitization process was an insurance provider; since investment in mortgage backed securities (and other related assets) carried some risk investors wanted insurance against default. The instrument that was used to provide insurance for such transactions was the credit default swap (CDS), a derivative financial instrument. Suppose

7. See http://www.investopedia.com/articles/03/102203.asp

an investor bought bonds worth $1 million; then, to insure herself against the possibility of default she could buy CDS from some financial firm like AIG on those bonds. The insurance premium that she had to pay, called the CDS rate or spread, was typically in the range of 1-2 percent of the value of the bonds, $1 million in this case. She would thus pay $ 20,000 (if the CDS rate was 2 percent) and the CDS contract would protect her against default for the period of the validity of the contract (typically a few years). In the bonds were to go into default the firm that had issued the CDS would have to pay her the amount of her losses.

There were several problems with the CDS market. First, it was an over-the-counter (OTC) market and did not operate through an exchange; hence the possibilities of monitoring or regulating this market were negligible. All the contracts were bilateral contracts and no one other than the two parties to the exchange could, in principle know the details of the contract. Second, unlike traditional insurance contracts, there were no reserve requirements. Thus, the financial entity selling the CDS was not required, by law, to hold any reserves against the CDS issued, unlike traditional insurance. So, if the CDS were to actually come due there was no guarantee that the firm that had issued the CDS would be in a situation to make good it's side of the contract. Third, the most bizarre aspect of the CDS market was that the investor buying the CDS was not required to hold the underlying assets.

This third aspect is truly incredible and led to a veritable explosion of speculation. Let us think about this for a minute. It meant that if an investor believed GM would fail three years down the line, she could buy $10 million worth of CDS on GM bonds by paying a fee of $200,000 (assuming a CDS rate of 2 percent); and this the investor could do even though she *did not* hold any GM bonds. If GM actually failed and her bet was correct she could make $10 million on an investment of $200,000, a phenomenal 49 fold return! One could never expect to make such return by actually holding the bonds, and so investors started making huge bets using the credit default swaps instead of investing in bonds and stocks. By the end of

2007, the CDS market had grown to about $ 55 trillion (about 4 times US gross domestic product).

But who bought the asset backed securities? Who bought the CDS? The short answer is: international investors of all kinds. Around the late 1990s, there was an enormous pool of footloose, speculative capital sloshing around in the global financial arena. The East Asian crisis, the Russian crisis and several other developing country crises freed up finance for investment in the US; and these investors wanted high returns even if that meant holding risky assets. That is precisely what the Wall Street investment banks were busy churning out: highly risky but high-return investments in the form of the asset backed securities and other more exotic assets like CDOs. Hedge funds, pension funds, sovereign wealth funds and other large institutional investors lapped up the exotic assets which promised high returns. Often the same investment bank that sold these assets also sold the credit default swaps, i.e., the insurance contract against default, too; this lulled the international investors into a false sense of security and they poured their funds into this high-risk-high-return game.

**The Credit Boom-Bust**

The medium term story about the house price bubble and the accompanying speculation using newly invented financial instruments like asset backed securities, collateralized debt obligations, and credit default swaps bears uncanny resemblance to the financial instability hypothesis that Hyman Minsky advanced long ago (Minsky, 1986). Minsky believed that financial instability was endogenously generated by the very logic of finance within capitalism. The process, according to Minsky, develops in five steps: displacement, boom, euphoria, profit-taking and bust.

Displacement is an event, set of events or abrupt policy change that draws the attention of investors and whets their appetite for taking risk. As funds are poured into assets, an asset price boom builds up and gives way to all round euphoria. A characteristic feature of this phase is the widespread belief, observed in the US for the past few years, that asset prices will keep moving up for a long time to come, if not forever. As euphoria takes hold of the economy, it infects banks and other financial institutions too. Under the tight grip of euphoria, banks become willing to make loans on much more easier terms that would have been thought possible even a few months or weeks ago. Easy credit leads to a huge build-up of leveraged positions.

Minsky distinguished between three different kinds of financial positions: hedge, speculative and ponzi. A hedge position is the safest one, where income flows in every future period is expected to cover payment commitments; a speculative position is a little more risky, because it entails rolling over debt for the periods in the near future with the implicit expectation to cover the debt build-up of the initial periods by large income flows sometime in the future. Ponzi positions are the most risky because it entails payment shortfalls, to be met by issuance of debt, for all but one period far away in the future; there is an implicit expectation of a huge payoff in a period very far off in the future that will then cover up all the initial debt build-up. With the availability of easy credit and an atmosphere of euphoria, the financial fragility of the economy increases, according to Minsky, because more and more hedge positions turn into speculative and speculative ones often turn into ponzi.

The highly-leveraged investment game, in this case mediated through asset backed securities and credit default swaps, could remain profitable if either of two conditions were met: (a) mortgage payments kept coming in, and (b) house prices kept moving up. If mortgage payments stopped coming in, the property could be taken over and sold; hence sub-prime mortgages remained profitable investments even when the borrower was almost certain to default as long as house prices kept moving up. In the middle of 2006 some savvy investors cashed in their profits and moved out; house prices stopped rising and foreclosures started piling up; and then the whole process, the whole speculative game, started unraveling. The US economy had very swiftly moved into a Minsky-bust, with all the attendant pain waiting down the road.

**Back to the Short Term Once Again**

With the medium term story more or less under our belts, let us return once more to the short term story and explore the details of some of the crucial moments. Let us, in other words, ask: why did Bear Stearns fail? Why did Lehman Brothers fail? Why was Fannie and and Freddie nationalized? What caused the near-collapse of AIG?

Bear Stearns and Lehman Brothers went under for very similar reasons: they could not keep borrowing to finance their positions; they had speculative positions, if one is permitted to use Minsky's terminology, and required to constantly meet the market to roll over their debt. Towards the end of it's life, Lehman was rolling over close to $ 100 billion a month to finance it's investments in real estate, stocks, asset-backed securities, bonds and other financial assets. This was of course extremely risky, and made the firm vulnerable to the fluctuations of the credit market. When news of foreclosures started pouring in, investors became convinced that Lehman had big holes in it's balance sheet because of it's exposure to the sub-prime mortgage market. They refused to lend it money for the fear of losing their investments; thus Lehman's cost of borrowing went up, it's stock prices plummeted and it's credit rating was dropped. With no other option left to fend off the fierce run on it's reserves, Lehman had to file for bankruptcy on September 15, 2008.

Fannie Mae and Freddie Mac were huge government supported entities (GSEs) that were created to help low-income homeowners get easy access to the mortgage market. They were meant to guarantee mortgages, thereby providing funds to the mortgage originators and providing incentives to firms for making loans to low-income homeowners. These GSEs were supposed to finance this operation by issuing it's own bonds which were implicitly backed by the US government making them highly valued by investors across the globe. It is now clear that Fannie and Freddie did not stick to this mandate of theirs. Instead, they used the implicitly subsidized loans that they could get from the market (due to the implicit government guarantee) to invest in mortgage backed securities which were backed by pools of sub-prime mortgages, mortgages they could not legally hold. When the foreclosures climbed and house prices started falling, sub-prime mortgages started failing, and these institutions started losing asset values; it became clear by mid-2007 that they could not sustain the mounting losses. At that point the government stepped in to explicitly guarantee their debt (because it was spread far and wide in the global financial system) which finally culminated in their nationalization in mid-September, 2008.

AIG, the largest insurance company in the US, got into serious trouble because of a different but related reason: the credit default swaps that it's London office had recklessly written. Around mid-September, about $ 57 billion of insurance contracts that it had written, in the form of CDS, required it to raise serious money. The CDS were all written on bonds linked to pools of sub-prime mortgages and as the sub-prime market worsened, the possibilities of the CDS payouts coming due increased. Because of the possible losses that it could incur, credit rating agencies downgraded AIG debt. The way the CDS contracts were written, a credit downgrade required AIG to demonstrate that it was capable of making good on it's CDS contracts should they come due; this required it to immediately "post collateral" to the tune of $ 15 billion. If it failed to post collateral, it would be considered bankrupt. Since it did not have that amount of reserves and could not borrow from a tightening credit market, it had to approach the Fed for funds.

### Bursting Bubble: Deleveraging and Deflation

An aspect of the whole build-up that made the unravelling especially painful was the stupendous amount of leverage in the financial system. When the bubble was inflating every investment was so hugely profitable that investors borrowed heavily for investing. This was especially true of the investment banks whose leverage (i.e., ratio of debt to equity) was about 30:1 by 2007; thus, for every dollar of equity these institutions had borrowed 30 dollars. And a large part of the borrowing was at the shortest end of the market. This meant that the investment banks had to continuously borrow from the market (usually roll over their debt) in order to keep financing their assets and investments. This made the system extremely fragile because any serious problem would lead to painful deleveraging (i.e., forcibly reducing debt by various means often involving serious financial loss due to fire-sale of assets) and possibly even asset price deflation, as Minsky had indicated.

As foreclosures picked up speed, house prices started moving down. Defaults on mortgage payments and falling house prices meant that the mortgage backed securities started losing value. Often this meant that when lenders came knocking on the doors for their funds, assets had to be sold at short notice and at low prices to cover debt payments coming due. A rush to sell assets often led to a further fall in the value of assets, even those not linked to mortgage backed securities, leading to worsening balance sheets in wider and wider circles. With bonds losing value and even facing default, the CDS contracts suddenly started coming into effect. Since CDS issuers like AIG had not held any reserves for such contingencies, they got into greater and greater difficulties as bonds insured by CDS contracts started failing.

Falling assets values meant that financial firms faced greater difficulty in borrowing from the market, partly because the value of assets that they could offer as collateral had already fallen. Falling collateral value often leads to increasing costs of borrowing in terms of higher interest rates. Difficulty is accessing funds gives another push to sell off assets to cover debt payments coming due, taking the spiral one step down. Deleveraging and an asset price deflation and a string of failures and rescues really led the financial system, in mid-September 2008, to completely lose faith in itself; it is this severe loss of confidence that manifested itself in the credit freeze.

# 5

# THE LONG TERM STORY: MINSKY AFTER MARX

The long term story, as I have already indicated, is a story about the rise and (possible) fall of neoliberalism. The Golden Age of Capitalism - the two and a half decades after the second World War - drew to a close by the late 1960s and global capitalism entered a period of structural crisis. The process of general capital accumulation is largely driven by current and expected trends of profitability of capital (measured by the rate of profit). When the rate of profit declines the process of capital accumulation slows down, heralding a period of crisis of capitalism. The rate of profit had peaked in the early-to-mid 1960s in both Europe and the USA; thereafter, the rate of profit continued to decline for the next decade and a half falling from a high of about 20 percent to a low of around 10 percent.

## Structural Crisis of Capitalism

Why did the rate of profit fall during this period? The falling profit rate goes to the heart of capitalism and shows up deep contradictions in the process of economic growth and technical change that accompanies capitalist development. The technological dynamism of capitalism is driven by competition between capitals to increase profits by reducing the cost of production. When the share of wages in national income is high, there is a strong incentive for capitalists to reduce the amount of labour required for production. The Golden Age of Capitalism, being a period of regulated and welfare capitalism, had ensured high and rising real wages and therefore maintained a high and relatively constant share of wages in national income. That provided the incentive for adopting labour saving technical change, i.e., adopting new techniques of production that required less and less labour per unit of output. Labour saving technical change increased the productivity of labour.

But the increasing productivity of labour came at a cost: falling productivity of capital or the output-capital ratio (the ratio of output to capital). Labour saving technical change, which increased labour productivity, was only achieved by replacing labour with capital, i.e., more and more labour was replaced by more and more machines in the process of production. This is one of the characteristic features that we often observe with capitalist development: mechanization and the increasing capital intensity of production. The use of more and more machines that increased labour productivity meant that every unit of output now required less labour but more capital; thus average labour productivity increased but average capital productivity fell.

This is the pattern of technical change, whereby labour productivity increases but capital productivity falls, that accompanies capitalist development during significant periods of time. This is also the way Marx had described the pattern of technical change under capitalism in his discussion of the process of general capital accumulation in Volume 1 of Capital. That is why economists Gerard Dumenil and Dominique Levy has called this pattern "trajectories à la Marx", and Duncan Foley and Thomas Michl has called it Marx-biased technical change. But what has this pattern of technical change got to do with the falling rate of profit?

The rate of profit is defined as the ratio of profits to the total stock of capital and can be decomposed as follows:

rate of profit = (profit/capital) = (profit/output)*(output/capital).

Thus we see that the rate of profit is the product of two crucial ratios: (1) the share of profits in output, and (2) the productivity of capital or the output-capital ratio. The share of profits in output had remained relatively stable through the Golden Age of Capitalism; this is a typical pattern observed under capitalism (other than for the neoliberal period). The productivity of capital, on the other hand, fell because of Marx-biased technical change leading to a sharp fall in the rate of profit, and ushering in a period of crisis for capitalism. The sharp decline in the rate of profit meant a decline in the revenues accruing to all sectors of the capitalist class, especially the top fraction. The neoliberal counterrevolution, the sharp turn in economic and social policy around the mid-1970s, was the response of the upper fraction of the capitalist class to their declining income and power[8].

**Neoliberal Response as Prelude to Crisis**

The neoliberal turn largely managed to achieve what it had set out to. Profit rates started moving up and the revenue accruing to capital, especially the top fraction of capital associated with the financial sector, increased enormously. But

**FIGURE 4 : PRODUCTIVITY INDEX (US Nonfarm Business: 1992=100)**

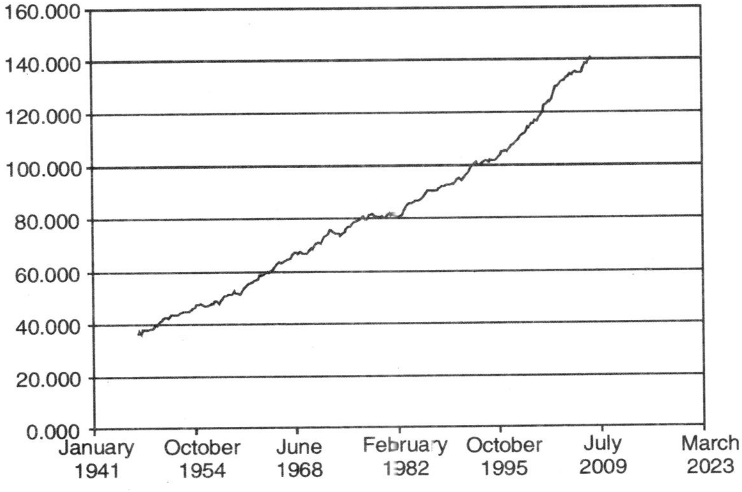


---

8. A more detailed development of this argument can be found in Dumenil and Levy, 2004.

it was a period of unmitigated disaster for the working class. Unemployment rates rose across the capitalist world, wages stopped growing (or slowed down considerably) in real terms, social welfare expenditures were gradually cut down, unions and other working class organizations were "busted"; in short, the social power and revenue accruing to the working class was severely restricted. It was a true counterrevolution which restored the power and privilege of the ruling class.

Figures 4 and 5 demonstrate this in vivid terms. Between 1950 and 1973, real wages had increased at an annual compound rate of 2.61 percent, closely following the phenomenal growth of labour productivity (which grew at an average annual compound rate of 2.70 percent). The next 25 years stand in stark contrast to this. Between 1974 and 1999, labour productivity grew at 1.62 percent per annum while real wages grew at only 0.92 percent per annum. Thus, even though labour productivity growth had slowed down significantly, it was still growing at close to twice rate at which real wages increased. This created a stupendous growth in profit incomes and created the source of finance that was to submerge the US working class in debt for the next four decades.

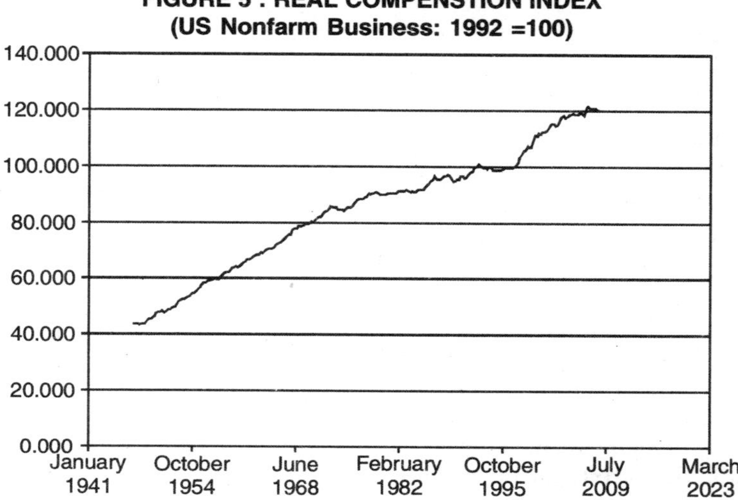

A crucial aspect of the neoliberal turn was the deregulation of sundry aspects of the economy, including, most importantly, the domain of operation of finance. The last great crisis of capital during the Great Depression had brought forth several important changes and new developments in the regulatory framework of capitalism. One by one, each of these laws relating to the operation of finance, both domestically and internationally, were whittled down or even outright overturned. Thus, the burgeoning profit income and the shredding of all regulation together created the supply of debt finance in the US economy. The demand for debt arose from a working class facing stagnant wage incomes but long used to growing consumption expenditures. The net result was the largest build-up of debt in the US economy since the Great Depression. During the beginning of the Great Depression total debt was about 300 percent of US GDP; in early 2008, total debt in the US economy was touching 350 percent of GDP. It was this huge debt build-up resulting from three decades of neoliberal economic policies that created a systemically fragile financial superstructure which imploded when the housing bubble burst[9].

In a sense, therefore, this was a Minsky-after-Marx crisis. The structural crisis of capitalism in the 1970s, a typical Marx-crisis, brought in the neoliberal counterrevolution. The neoliberal counterrevolution, in turn, created the conditions for the emergence and consolidation of speculative finance capital. The irrational exuberance accompanying the speculative build-up, a phenomenon that Hyman Minsky had studied in great detail[10], gradually created a financially fragile economy and led us on to this Minsky-crisis.

---

9. I have borrowed parts of this argument from Wolff, 2008.
10. See this interesting article: http://www.newyorker.com/talk/comment/2008/02/04/080204taco_talk_cassidy

# REFERENCES

Dumenil, G. and D. Levy. 2004. *Capital Resurgent: Roots of the Neoliberal Revolution*. Harvard University Press.

Minsky, H. 1986. *Stabilizing an Unstable Economy*. Yale University Press.

Wolff. R. 2008. *Capitalism Hits the Fan*. Available at: http://www.alternet.org/workplace/105944/capitalism_hits_the_fan/